D1560391

By Rachel Lynette • Illustrated by Mernie Gallagher-Cole

The Child's World

Published by The Child's World®
1980 Lookout Drive • Mankato, MN 56003-1705
800-599-READ • www.childsworld.com

Acknowledgments
The Child's World®: Mary Berendes, Publishing Director
The Design Lab: Design and production
Red Line Editorial: Editorial direction

Design elements: Billyfoto/Dreamstime;
Dan Ionut Popescu/Dreamstime

ISBN 9781614732662
LCCN 2012932872

Printed in the United States of America
Mankato, MN
July 2012
PA02117

About the Author: Rachel Lynette has written more than 100 books for children as well as resources for teachers. She uses dozens of punctuation marks every day. Without them, she could not do her job! Rachel's favorite punctuation mark is the exclamation point!

About the Illustrator: Mernie Gallagher-Cole is a freelance children's book illustrator living outside of Philadelphia. She has illustrated many children's books. Mernie enjoys punctuation marks so much that she uses a hyphen in her last name!

It was a bright morning in Punctuation Junction. Super C was ready to start his day. But first he needed his breakfast. A nice bowl of Super Hero Flakes sounded good. One thing was missing, though. Super C was out of milk! There was only one thing to do. Super C had to go to Super Foods.

Super C saw that something was very wrong at the store. No punctuation were picking things off the shelves. Nothing was in their carts. Each punctuation held a nearly blank piece of paper.

Then Susie the apostrophe spotted Super C. "Help us, Super C," she said. "All of our shopping lists are blank. We do not know what to buy."

Super C took a closer look at Susie's list. There were no items listed. "How strange," said Super C. "I wonder what is going on."

Ring! Ring! Super C answered his cell phone. It was the Mayor. "Super C, I do not know what to do!" he yelled. "My important jobs list is blank! I wrote it last night. I looked at my list today. Everything is gone."

"Oh dear, this is a problem," said Super C.

"And this morning Counselor Bob called me," said the mayor. "All the children showed up for camp. But they did not have their camping gear. Bob had given each camper a list of what to bring, though. Help us, Super C!"

"I think I know what is wrong. The colons are missing!" Super C said. "I'm sending a letter to you now. Make sure everyone in Punctuation Junction gets it. I have to find out where the colons are."

Attention all punctuation!

Your lists disappeared because the colons are missing! A colon is used to connect a sentence to a list. The items on a list drop off without a colon. No one should make lists until I return.

A colon is used in other ways, too. It connects parts of sentences. And you use a colon before a quote. This tells you what someone said.

As you can see, colons are very important! I'll be back with all the colons soon.

Sincerely,
Super C

Super C used his super powers to bounce. He went high into the sky. He flew above all of the buildings. Super C looked all around for the missing colons. Then he saw something he had not seen before. On the edge of town was a roller coaster. In fact, it was a whole carnival!

It took Super C three jumps to get to the carnival. A large sign stood outside a locked gate. Inside he could hear music and colons on rides. Super C was just about to bounce over the fence. But Evil Pete stopped him.

"I should have known it was you!" said Super C. "But why did you take all the colons?"

"I did not take them!" said Evil Pete. "I just told them about the Colon Carnival. They came running. Colons love a good carnival, you know."

"That's true, " said Super C. "But now the colons must come home."

"I am afraid that is where I draw the line," said Evil Pete. "The colons stay here. *Muah-ha-ha-ha-ha!*" He ended with an evil laugh.

"I do not think so, Evil Pete," Super C said as he bounced into the air. He landed on Evil Pete's side. He pushed Evil Pete's point into the ticket office. Evil Pete was stuck!

Soon the colons came up to Super C. "You must return to Punctuation Junction! We need you there!" Super C told them.

The colons bounced back to town. The things on everyone's lists showed up again. The mayor got all his important jobs done.

The camp kids all returned to camp. But this time they brought their sleeping bags and fishing poles. It was just what Counselor Bob wanted them to bring.

Susie finished her shopping. And Super C finally bought his milk. "Yum!" he said as he sat down to what was now a tasty lunch.

PUNCTUATION FUN

Now that the colons are back, they need help finding where they belong. Add a colon to each sentence. Remember, the colon connects a complete sentence to a list or an explanation.

1. These are some of the people that live in Punctuation Junction Susie, the mayor, and Super C.
2. Evil Pete only has one thing on his mind kidnapping all the colons.
3. This is what Super C did he rescued the colons.
4. When all of the colons were missing, the mayor knew just who to call Super C.
5. Evil Pete an evil villain!

DO NOT WRITE IN THE BOOK!

FUN FACTS

After http, Please!

Did you know colons help you find Web sites? They are an important part of Web addresses. You put them right after the http.

Just Like a Limb

The word *colon* comes from a Greek word. It means *limb*. A limb is a smaller part of something that sticks out from the main part. A colon connects the main part of a sentence (or the trunk) to the end (or limb).

What's the Time?

Colons are used when writing the time, such as 8:30. They separate the hours from the minutes.

A Pause, Not a Stop

The colon was once used like a period. It marked the end of a sentence. The letter following the colon was always a capital letter. But its use changed through time. Now it marks the beginning of a list, quote, or summary.

Between Names

Ben Jonson was an English author from the 1600s. His book *The English Grammar* explained how the colon should be used. Jonson liked the colon so much, he added it to his name. He wrote his name as Ben:Jonson.